Rebekah Smith

CW00494893

KS1 History

STEP BACK IN TIME

Photocopiable Activity Book

Our First
Six Years

Toys
'NOW' and 'THEN'

Seaside Holidays
Long Ago

Homes
'NOW' & 'THEN'

When Gran &
Grandad
Were Young

Castles
Long Ago

by Jean E. Fone & Pat Lamb

Introduction

The aim of this book is to provide resources to help Key Stage 1 teachers introduce elements of local and recent historical events to their pupils.

Subjects studied in this book are:

Our First Six Years
Toys – 'Now' and 'Then'
When Gran and Grandad Were Young
Seaside Holidays – Long Ago
Homes – 'Now' and 'Then'
Castles – Long Ago

Detailed notes provide background information about each topic to be studied. Teacher's notes explain the purpose of each photocopiable activity page.

The photocopiable activities include: shared texts; pictures from the past; timelines; study of artefacts; 'Now' and 'Then' activities; puzzles; jig-saws and models to make. Simple assessment sheets at two different levels are provided at the back of the book.

The authors would like to thank all those who have loaned personal photographs for this book. The authors and publishers would like to thank the following for permission to use images:

Salmon Picture Library for photographs on page 36 and 57.

Mary Evans Picture Library for 'New Baby' on page 50 and 'Arrow Pierces Eye 1066' on page 56.

Fine Art Photographs for 'Washing Day' on page 50.

Topical Resources
P.O. Box 329
Broughton
Preston
Lancashire
PR3 5LT

Topical Resources publishes a range of Educational Materials for use in Primary Schools and Pre-School Nurseries and Playgroups.

For the latest catalogue:
Tel: 01772 863158
Fax: 01772 866153
e.mail: sales@topical-resources.co.uk
Visit our Website at: www.topical-resources.co.uk

Copyright © 2005 Jean E. Fone & Pat Lamb
Illustrated by John Hutchinson
Typeset by 'ArtWorks', 69 Worden Lane, Leyland PR25 3BD Tel: 01772 431010
Printed in Great Britain for 'Topical Resources' by T. Snape & Company Ltd., Boltons Court, Preston, Lancashire.

Published May 2005

ISBN 1 872977 90 1

Contents

Our First Six Years

Thinking about ourselves is a popular topic, helping children to understand their place in history. The following activities focus on the changes and differences which have happened in the lives of six year olds over the last hundred years. In particular the use of primary source material has been deemed to be important. Photographs of children and their parents give some indication how life has changed over the last hundred years.

At the beginning of the twentieth century, six year olds were dressed very differently. Life in general was more formal including clothes. Best clothes were kept for high days and holidays. The Education Act of 1870 gave the opportunity for most children to be engaged in some form of schooling. The curriculum consisted mainly in teaching children how to read, write and do arithmetic. Slates and sand were used for the beginning of writing and then children continued at a later stage with pen and ink and probably many blots and blobs!

Children born during and after the Second World War experienced a time of shortages and rationing. Coupons were required for both clothing and food. However, in spite of this, life could still be fun. Very few people had a television. There were no computers or videos. In the evenings the family played games such as ludo, snakes and ladders or made models with Meccano. New toys only appeared on special occasions such as Christmas and birthdays. Sometimes toys were home-made; clothes knitted for dolls and wooden toys made by parents. During the daytime children in towns and cities played in the street with skipping ropes, two or three balls thrown against the wall, hide and seek, whip and top which entailed keeping a box of coloured chalks with which to decorate the top. Five stones was played with five stones on the back of your hand, throwing them in the air and catching as many as you could. In the countryside many similar games were played but children were free to play games in the barns and safely go out for the day to fish and explore. Attending the cinema was popular entertainment both before and after the war. For a treat sometimes an ice cream was allowed, often in a little tub with a wooden spoon. As books were expensive many young children were taken to the library. Comics were popular too – The Dandy or Beano for younger children and then Eagle or School Friend for older children.

The paper shortage during the war meant that comics only came out fortnightly.

Some families were lucky enough to go to the seaside for an annual holiday. Many of the men wore caps on the beach and wore the same clothes they wore on a normal day. Bathing costumes for women were often made of wool.

In 1953 many six year olds enjoyed the Coronation of Queen Elizabeth 11. Televisions were few so people gathered together to watch the great event. Street parties were held all over the country. Many children were given souvenirs of the event. Children could ask older adults if they still have their Coronation mugs or glasses. I wonder how many were dropped on the way home from school!

1953 Coronation Glass –inscribed on one side, 'County Borough of Stockport', and on the other, 'ER Coronation of Queen Elizabeth II, 2nd June 1953'.

Additional Activities

1   Make a display of clocks to show the passing of time. Are there other ways in which people could tell the time? e.g. sundials, water clocks, candle clocks etc.

2   Provide a selection of books to show how children lived in the past and encourage them to do their own research.

3   Use a mirror and make observational drawings of your own face using a variety of media.

4   Make a large wall collage of faces to celebrate the diversity of people in the world. Or make two collages, one showing children of the world the other showing adults. Talk about what life will be like in the future when the children are adults.

Our First Six Years

The following activities can be used as shared texts by enlarging to A3 size.

page

5 History Starts With Me

An opportunity for children to discuss what it is like to be six and note the changes in dress and hairstyles over the past hundred years. Joe was six just after the second world war. Kirsty was six in 2004. Frank was six at the beginning of the 20th century. Neil was six in 1996.

Discuss the differences in clothes and pose. Make a timeline and place on it these four children and pictures of others you have collected. Count in tens and then discuss the word century. Make a display of six year olds you know.

6 At Last I am Six

Born in 1942, Emma's development is shown in a series of photographs from 6 months, 1 year, 2 years and 6 years old – all were taken in black and white. Put the pictures in order. Discuss the clothes, dress styles, baby's pram and toys of the period. Ask children to bring in photographs of themselves at the same ages and make comparisons. Use the booklet on page 11 in order to make sequenced stories of their own lives.

7 Six Year Olds at School

Compare the two class-rooms – one at the end of the nineteenth century and the other in the twenty first century. How are they different in terms of dress styles, the formality of the classroom and technology? Compare your own class-room. Make pairs of drawings – 'NOW' and 'THEN' to show the comparisons, e.g. show how the children are seated, how they are dressed. Place captions beneath each picture. Look in books to

page

find out the kind of equipment used in the past. Study the photographs below to observe children at play at the present time.

8 When I Was Young

In the ovals on the left hand side of the page draw your own face as a baby, a toddler and at six years old. Now write about what you could do at each stage. In the picture boxes draw yourself or obtain a photograph which shows each stage of development.

9 What Shall I do Today?

Look at the photograph of the six year old fifty years ago. Now draw yourself in the oval. Look at and discuss the photographs and illustrations of leisure activities of fifty years ago. In the spaces provided either draw or write about your leisure time today e.g. next to the ludo photograph write or draw about an indoor game you play today. Discuss, is it safe to play in the street today? Where do you play out of doors? Do you watch TV rather than listen to the radio? The 'Annual' was a great treat. Paper was in short supply and books were expensive. What kind of books do you receive at Christmas time?

10 Mums and Dads With Their Children

Discus the parents and the four children in the photographs and the four captions and then involve pupils in each of the activities indicated on the captions. Jane was born during the second world war. George was born at the end of the nineteenth century. Alfred was born pre second world war. Luke was born in 2003.

page

11 Growing Up

After folding the paper into sections, the outline can be cut out to form a mini book. Children can draw themselves on the front cover, and then put appropriate titles on the following pages in order to draw and write about sequenced events in their lives – thus forming their own timelines. Alternatively books could be made entitled, 'Games I Play,' 'My Family and Friends' or 'My School Life.' Look also at the activity on page 6.

12 When was a Long Time Ago?

An activity which will allow children to discuss, draw, write and understand more about the passage of time. Create a 'Long Ago' board and invite children to find other words which elude to the way in which time passes – e.g. century, decade, year, season, while, breakfast, lunch, tea, dinner, supper, etc.

Key Vocabulary

Long ago, yesterday, last night, the week before, soon, tomorrow, old, older, toddler, baby, teenager and growing up.

History Starts With Me

Look at us! We are Kirsty, Joe, Frank and Neil. We are all 6-years old. Are any of us dressed like you?

I am Joe

I am Kirsty

I am Frank

I am Neil

At Last I Am Six

Look at me! My name is Emma. Here I am when I was six-months old, 1 year old, 2 years old and 6 years old. Put my pictures in order.

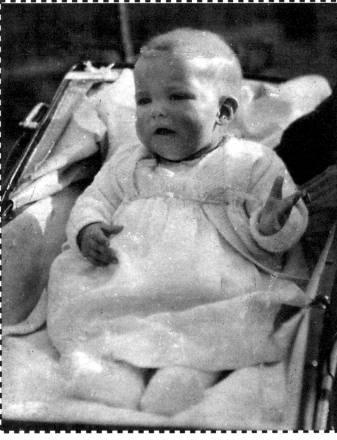

Six Years Old and at School - 'Then' & 'Now'

What difference can you see between these two classrooms?
Which is most like your classroom?

When I Was Young

When I was a baby
I could

Here I am as a baby.

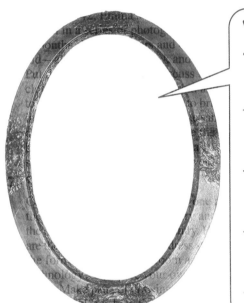

When I was a
toddler I could

Here I am as a toddler

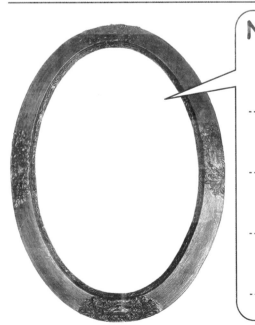

Now I am six I can

Here I am 6 years old.

What Shall I Do Today?

Here are some of the things I liked to do fifty years ago when I was six.

Now I am six, here are some of the things I like to do.

I played Ludo by the fireside.

I played hopscotch in the street.

I listened to the radio.

I had an annual for my Christmas present.

Mums and Dads With Their Children

Look at the children and their Mums and Dads. What differences can you see in the photographs? Which baby was born in the 21st century? How do you know?

Here is George with his Mum. He is six-years old. This picture was taken 100-years ago. Draw pictures of how girls and boys were dressed long ago.

Here is Jane with her Dad. What will she look like when she is six-years old? Draw her portrait.

Here is Alfred with his Mum and Dad. Alfred was a baby 70-years ago. What will he look like now?

Here is Luke with his Mum. He is a one-year old. How will he be dressed when he is 6?

4

5

3

6

2

7

Title

by

1

When Was a Long Time Ago?

Draw pictures from the past.

Ten minutes ago	An hour ago	Before Breakfast
Last Night	Yesterday	Last Week

Draw pictures about the future.

Soon	Tomorrow	Next Year

Toys - 'Now' & 'Then'

Toys or playthings for the use of children not only bring amusement and entertainment, but are an aid to education and can influence their social, emotional and physical development.

Early Moving Toys

In the 18th and 19th centuries mechanical toys, with moving parts, became very popular and there were many types of such toys. Some were simple, like walking dolls or balancing toys. Others were more complicated, made with great detail, had clockwork power, and were often for adult amusement.

The 'pantin' was one of the most popular children's toys ever and soon became a source of entertainment for grown-ups too. It was a figure, usually a clown or a dancer, with arms which could rotate and move at the shoulders and hips. When the string was pulled at the top and bottom, the arms and legs moved up and down.

Early Optical Toys

Optical toys were popular with both children and adults. They used light, mirrors and movement to create optical effects and illusion. The Kaleidoscope - a toy still available today - was invented in 1818. It consists of a tube, with an eye-hole at one end, and a box containing mirrors and pieces of glass at the other. By rotating this box, beautiful and colourful symmetrical patterns are produced. The first kaleidoscopes were made with brass cases and glass lenses. They had the appearance more of scientific instruments. The introduction of plastic lenses made them cheaper and more robust.

The Zoetrope, which appeared in the 1860's, was another favourite optical toy. It was a spinnable drumlike cylinder with slits all around the circumference. A series of pictures was placed on the inside of the drum. As the child spun the drum, and looked at the pictures on the opposite side through the slits, the pictures appeared to move. The picture strips showed such things as birds in flight, acrobats, jugglers and dancers, often in cartoon form, and could be replaced to show a new set of moving pictures.

The Thaumatrope was one of the earliest and simplest of optical toys. It consisted of a stiff, paper disc with a string on both ends. A different picture was drawn on both sides of the disc, e.g.a flower on one side and a pot on the other. Spinning the disc made the two pictures appear to come together and form one picture. The eye continues to 'see' an image for a moment after it has disappeared. The thaumatrope spins faster than the eye works, so you can 'see' the pictures on both sides at once.

Jigsaw Puzzles

Jigsaw puzzles are a pastime, which bring a great deal of entertainment, in a group, or as a solitary activity. They are educational and recyclable, in that when completed they can be broken up and done again.

Jigsaw puzzles were first produced, in about 1760, by a map-maker called John Spilsbury, as an educational aid for geography. He put his map on a piece of hardwood and cut around the borders of the countries with a fine-bladed marquetry saw. These puzzles were known as 'dissections'.

In 1880, with the introduction of the treadle saw, they became known as jigsaw puzzles. Pictures were painted or glued onto plywood, and pencil tracings made on the back to show where to cut. In the late 19th century, cardboard was introduced for children's puzzles. These were 'die-cut'. Thin strips of metal with sharp edges are twisted into patterns and fastened to a plate. This is the 'die'. The die is placed in a press and then pressed down onto cardboard to make the cut.

Jigsaw puzzles reached their height of popularity in the 1920's and 1930's. Chad Valley and Victory were popular British manufacturers, producing jigsaw puzzles in both cardboard and wood, of sentimental scenes and other topical subjects, such as trains, boats etc.

Development of Toys in the 20th Century

The 20th century saw new developments in toy making and the use of new materials. It included soft toys, construction toys and wheeled toys. With the introduction of the 'Teddy Bear' in 1903, other soft cuddly toys, such as rabbits, pandas and golliwogs appeared and are as popular as ever today. Plastic became a widely used material after the Second World War. With the introduction of 'Bakelite' and later vinyls, the bodies of dolls began to look more realistic. 'Meccano' was the first major success in construction toys in 1901. It was made of metal pieces in a variety of shapes which could be screwed together. There are now a great variety of such toys which appeal to the creative instincts of both boys and girls. The most popular of these is Lego, an interlocking construction toy made of plastic, which won Toy of the Year in1974. It was invented in 1932 by Ole Christiansen, a Danish man. The word 'Lego' comes from two Danish words 'Leg Godt' which mean 'play well' in English.

A 100 Years of Popular Toys

1903	Introduction of first 'crayola` crayons.
1925	The first 'Hornby' electric trains.
1928	Mickey Mouse was created by Walt Disney; the first licenced toy.
1929	Yo-yos were launched.
1931	Scrabble was invented.
1936	Monopoly was invented by the Parker brothers in U.S.A.
1949	Lego was launched.
1952	The first 'matchbox' car was introduced.
1956	'Scalectrix' appeared in the shops.
1959	Barbie was created by Ruth Hander and was named after her daughter.
1966	'Action Man', the first boy's doll, became a great success.
1971	Spacehoppers, inflatable orange bouncers with horns for handles, were all the rage.
1975	The 'Wombles' were introduced.
1978	Star Wars toys dominated toy shops after the film release and were popular until mid1980's.
1982	BMX bikes were the thing to have.
1985	Transformers, robots in disguise, transformed from vehicle to robot and back again.
1990	Teenage Mutant Hero Turtles arrived in the shops.
1991	Nintendo launched 'Game Boy'.
1993	Power Rangers, toys based on the television show, were an immediate hit.
1997	The year of the Teletubbies.
2001	Bob the Builder was the big hit.
2002	Bratz dolls were introduced.

Bicycles and Tricycles

Juvenile bicycles and tricycles are designed for children and are smaller versions of adult models. Cycling is a good form of physical exercise and enables children to get out and about.

In the 1870's the 'Penny-farthing' or 'high-wheeler' appeared. It had a huge front wheel and a small rear one. The frontwheel in some models was 1.5 metres high. Each turn of the pedal turned the large wheel round once, so the bike travelled a long way with just one turn of the pedal.

The tricycle was popular for children from the 1900's and was a safe introduction to cycling for youngsters. Nowadays, the two-wheeler with stabilisers has taken its place. The 'Chopper' bike appeared in American stores in 1963 and was an overnight success. The design was influenced by motorbikes with big 'ape-hanger' handlebars and rear mudguard cut in half. The 'Raleigh Rodeo' was every boys dream with it's 20 inch wheels, ape-hangers and long seat.

Bicycles of today are manufactured in various styles and sizes. Popular types are mountain, BMX, and freestyle.

Toys - 'Now' and 'Then'

Page

15 Days Gone By -
Make a Timeline

Enlarge the activity page onto A3 and use for discussion with the children. How can they tell the photographs are old? Talk about the styles of clothes and, most importantly, the toys that the boys and girls are holding. Describe the differences/similarities with toys today.

Suggested activities include: Make a class timeline, 1900 to present day, of children with their toys. Cut out the photographs on the page and arrange in sequence on the timeline. Encourage the children to bring in photographs from home of grandparents, parents, themselves with toys and add to the timeline. OR Use a digital camera to take an image of one of the children with a toy train, skipping rope, doll and pram, and compare with those on the activity page. Have available some old sepia photos to show the children and compare with the digitally produced image. Children draw and paint a 'sepia' picture showing a child with a toy.

16 Moving Toys -
Make a Pantin

Refer to teacher's notes to inform the children about the 'pantin', which was one of the most popular toys ever.

1 Copy the activity page on to thin card. Colour and cut out carefully.

2 Pierce holes on the body and limbs where indicated.(Children might need help with this.)

3 Make the limbs swing easily using brass-coloured paper fasteners.

4 Attach strings to the legs and arms as shown.

5 Pull the bottom string and watch the clown move his arms and legs.

17 An Optical Toy -
Make a Thaumatrope

The background notes give information on early optical toys, such as the thaumatrope and zoetrope, and explain how they work. Make comparisons with modern computer games etc. Follow the instructions to make a thaumatrope on the activity page .

Have available, if possible, a kaleidescope for the children to examine and use. This is an optical toy invented in 1818, and still available today.

page

18 Sort the Toys into'Now' and 'Then'

This activity gives teachers and children the opportunity to discuss some of the differences and similarities in toys past and present. Have available pictures, books and photographs of toys in the 1950's for the children to study and make comparisons with present day toys. Draw attention to design, materials and how the toys move as well as appearance. Use the pictures on the activity page to make a zig-zag booklet (see page 11) with NOW pictures on one side and THEN pictures on the other. The children could add drawings/pictures of their own to each side.

Encourage the children to bring in toys that grandparents/ parents had when they were little and make a class museum. The toys could be arranged in a three dimensional timeline on a shelf.

19 Draw and Write About a Special Toy

Look at, and discuss the photograph of the little boy with Father Christmas and the toys he received. Explain that it is about fifty years old. What do the children think of the toys and would they have liked them? Ask if any of them have visited Father Christmas and to relate their experiences. Did Father Christmas look the same? What gifts did they receive? On what other occasions have they been given a special toy?

The children go on to complete the activity sheet by drawing a picture and writing about a toy that they received as a present on a special occasion.

20 1950's Toys -
A Jigsaw to Make

Refer to the teacher's notes for information on the history and development of jigsaws. Talk about the jigsaw, which is original source material, and explain that this is the jigsaw that the little boy in the picture on page 19 received as a Christmas present.

Cut out the jigsaw pieces, make up the jigsaw and colour carefully.

How can the children tell that it is an old-fashioned jigsaw puzzle? Is it very different from ones used in the classroom now. The toy dress doll (page 18) and the card game (page 30) are both 1950's toys and could be used with this activity.

page

21 Sequencing Activity -
Out and About Looking at Bicycles

The aim of the activity is to give the children the opportunity to look at and discuss the two bicycles and the tricycle and to put them in sequence. Teacher's notes give details of the 'penny farthing' and the development of bicycles. Enlarge the activity page and ask the children to talk about the differences/similarities of the bicycles and tricycle, drawing their attention to the design, materials and how they move.

Either, children sketch the bicycles and tricycle, using the photographs as reference, or children draw a picture of themselves and in a speech bubble complete the sentence, I would like/ not like to ride the...because...

Children could investigate/collect pictures of other types of distinctive bicycles, such as the 'chopper' bicycle, and include them in their timeline.

Key Vocabulary

New, old, before, after, a long time ago, old-fashioned, past, present, fifty years ago, 1950's, days gone by. Sepia photograph, pantin, optical toy, thaumatrope, zoetrope, kaleidoscope, tricycle, penny-farthing

Additional Activities

1 Arrange a visit to a toy museum.

2 Make picture lists of 'old toys', toddler's toys, plastic/wooden toys.

3 Look at, and discuss, pictures by famous artists that depict children with toys, e.g. 'Bubbles' by John Everett Millais.

Days Gone By - Make a Timeline

Look carefully at the photographs of the girls and boys with their toys.
How can you tell that they are old? Do you have toys like these?

Frank with his toy train. 1905

Hilda and Evelyn
with their skipping rope. 1910

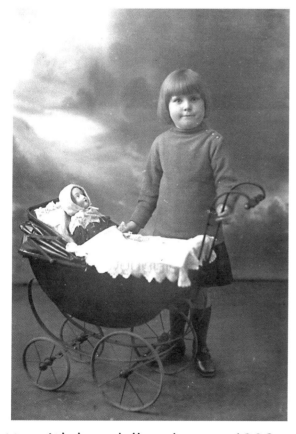

Betty with her doll and pram. 1920

Edward with his toy gun and holster.
1955

Draw a picture of yourself with your favourite toy. Put it on the timeline.

Moving Toys - Make a Pantin

The 'Pantin' was one of the most popular early moving toys.
You can use the template below to make a pantin of your own.

An Optical Toy - Make a Thaumatrope

The thaumatrope was one of the earliest and simplest toys that produces moving pictures. To make one you need: a piece of card, scissors, pencil/crayons, two pieces of string.

Draw a circle about 10cm across on the card and cut out.

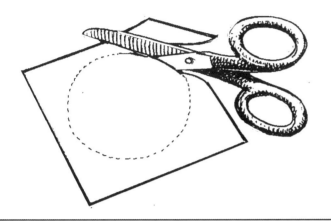

Make two holes on opposite sides of the circle. Tie a piece of string through each hole.

Draw a picture on one side of the circle.

Turn the circle over and upside-down. Now draw the rest of your picture.

Hold the string in your hands and wind up the circle tightly. When you release the circle it will spin and form a picture as the one below.

Sort the Toys into 'Now' and 'Then'

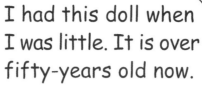

I had this doll when I was little. It is over fifty-years old now.

NOW

THEN

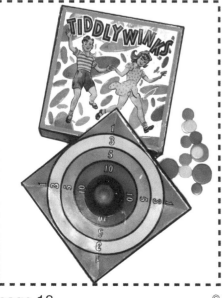

Draw and Write About a Special Toy

I visited Father Christmas when I was a boy. I was very excited. Here are some of the toys I asked for.

Draw and write about a toy that you had as a present on a special occasion.

_____

_____

_____

_____

_____

_____

A 1950's Jigsaw For You To Make

This is a jigsaw I had for Christmas. It is over 50-years old. Can you do it?

Out and About - Looking at Bicycles

Here are photographs of children's cycles. Look at them carefully. Can you tell which one is the oldest? Make a list of the differences.

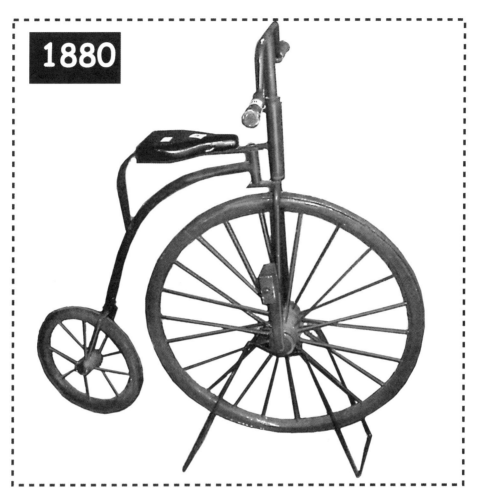

1880

1940

2004

Which bicycle do you think would be the most exciting to ride?

When Gran and Grandad Were Young

It is interesting to note that even children have stereotyped ideas of what gran and grandad look like and what they do. Gran is old and wrinkly with grey hair, and she bakes, sews and knits, whilst grandad is going bald, wears glasses, does the gardening and uses a walking stick. However, by looking at photographs and discussion, they soon realise that many grandparents do not fit the stereotypical image. Grandparents are often quite young, fashionable and very active.

It is important to talk about age to help the children to understand that older people have many more years in their lives and that gran and grandad were themselves children and parents. In the same way the children themselves will grow up and may be parents and grandparents too. Photographs are an important aid to information on families and their structure. They can be used to make a pictorial family tree and to illustrate the differences between past and present.

What Did They Wear?

The 1950's and 1960's, when many grandparents were children, was still a time when many children wore 'homemade' clothes. Coats, dresses, trousers etc. were made on old treadle sewing machines, or by hand, by mum or gran, who were often experts at embroidery and smocking. The more affluent children often had clothes made to measure by a dressmaker. Many children had a school outfit, a 'best' outfit and wore old clothes for playing out in. Cardigans, jumpers, hats, scarves, gloves and even socks were knitted at home. Old knitted garments were unravelled and the wool reused to make new ones, with odd bits of wool being saved to darn holes in socks and elbows. Clothes which were outgrown were passed down to siblings or given to other family members and friends. Sewing and knitting patterns could be bought from shops and were often featured in popular ladies' magazines.

School Life

The way children learn and what they learn has changed a lot in the last fifty years. School life was different for our grandparents with education being still very formal. Buildings were often old and dark, with high windows and poor heating. Children sat in desks in rows and worked in silence.

This is what one gran says about her life in the infant classes, "I attended school in a small rural Welsh town. The school building was built of stone and resembled a chapel with high windows. The toilets were in a shed at the bottom of the playground. An open fire heated the babies (4 to 5 years)

class and the other two classrooms were heated by a large cast-iron stove, which burned coke. In winter, our mid-morning milk was kept warm in a large saucepan on top of the stove.

The teacher stood behind a large desk in front of the blackboard and we sat in individual desks with pop-up seats. My teachers were very strict and anyone not paying attention or misbehaving was brought out to the front of the class and smacked on the hand with a ruler. We read aloud to the teacher in turn and no new book was started until everyone could read the current book. I remember in arithmetic reciting the times tables with the whole class until everyone was word perfect. The infants made raffia mats and played with Plasticine as a treat.

I loved nature lessons. We went for walks on the hills and in the woods, collecting wild flowers, such as bluebells. We always had a jar of frog-spawn every year and waited patiently for the tadpoles to appear.

There were no school dinners and most of us went home for lunch. Children from the farms who couldnt go home brought their own and sat at desks to eat it.

Our playground was behind the school and divided into 'girls' and 'boys' with a line down the middle. We girls played 'What time is it Mr. Wolf?', had skipping ropes and played hop-scotch. The boys played football, marbles and conkers in the autumn. They also wrestled a lot in the playground.

There was no television, computers or toys to play with but I had lots of fun and really enjoyed school."

Pre-Decimal Coins

Before the currency was decimalised in 1971 Britain had a variety of coins. Prices were quantified in pounds, shillings and pence. The halfpenny (ha'penny) was half a penny. It was last minted in 1967 and not in circulation at the time of decimilisation. There were twelve pennies in one shilling. There were three pennies in a 'thrupence'. It was a brass coin with twelve sides. The sixpence, the smallest silver coin was worth six pennies. There were twelve pennies in a shilling (often called a 'bob') and twenty shillings in pound. The florin, or two shilling piece, was worth two shillings, and a half crown was worth two shilling and six pence. The coins were recorded as follows: halfpenny =1/2d, penny = 1d, threepence = 3d, sixpence = 6d, shilling = 1/-, florin = 2/-, half-a-crown = 2/6. The farthing, last minted in 1957, was worth a quarter of a penny but was little used in the 1950's.

Parties

Parties were a special treat for children and were held in the house or the garden. Children attended in their best party clothes, - the girls in frilly party dresses with ribbons in their hair and the boys in short trousers and jacket and tie. Food usually consisted of paste or egg sandwiches cut into triangles, small cakes with icing on, the birthday cake and jelly and blanc mange. All of this would have been made by mum or gran at home. Familiar games such as 'pass the parcel', 'musical chairs' and 'pin the tail on the donkey' were played. Parents kept a close watch on proceedings and best behaviour and good manners at the table were expected from the children.

A Recipe for Peppermint Creams

This easy to make old-fashioned recipe for peppermint creams is another that the children might like to try.

You need: one packet of icing sugar, the white of an egg, green or pink food colouring and peppermint flavouring.

Sprinkle some icing sugar on a board.

Mix the egg white with the remaining icing sugar, peppermint flavouring and food colouring in a bowl until it makes a nice consistency. Add a little water carefully if necessary.

Divide the mixture into equal balls and form into a flat shape OR roll out the mixture onto the icing sugar on the board and cut into fancy shapes.

Allow to harden.

For information on games and toys - see teacher's background notes on Toys.

When Gran and Grandad Were Young

Page

24 Grandad's Timeline
A Sequencing Activity

The photographs are original source material and the aim is for the children to sequence the life of Grandad by looking at, and discussing the photographs of him at different ages in his life. The children can make a zig-zag booklet (see page 11). Cut out the photographs and stick them in order, matching the captions to the pictures. Encourage the children to design an appropriate cover for their booklet.

25 and 26 What Did They Wear?-
Dress the Dolls

Have available pictures and photographs of children in the 1950's and 1960's, dressed for different occasions, weather, etc. and make comparisons with the clothes children wear today. Refer to the teacher's background notes for more information on clothes. Discuss the fact that many clothes were homemade and that children passed them down to siblings. The aim is to give the children the opportunity to cut out and dress two dolls, giving an insight into the clothes worn by children in the 1950's.

The children could make a collection of old knitting and sewing patterns for a class display.

27 Grandad at School-
'Now' and 'Then' Activity

This is an ideal opportunity to invite Gran or Grandad into the class to talk to the children.

Enlarge the activity sheet onto A3, or put on an OHP, and use as a shared text for discussion. Encourage the children to make comparisons with their classrooms, equipment and routines, highlighting the similarities and differences, and to form opinions on their grandparents' school life. Background notes give information about school life in a rural Welsh town in the 1950's. A suggested activity for follow-up can be to make a 'Now And Then' booklet. Fold a piece of A4 paper in half and staple in the centre. The outer sheet can be made into a cover with a title and the left hand pages can be labelled 'THEN' and the right hand pages labelled 'NOW'. The children can cut out three pictures from the activity sheet and stick them onto the 'THEN' pages of their booklet and on the corresponding 'NOW' pages draw and write about what they use in their modern day classroom instead.

page

28 Make Gran's Purse

Have available a selection of pre-decimal coins for the children to examine. Compare the decimal coins and discuss the difference. Hold three old pennies in your hand. What do they feel like? Talk about comparative values of the old and new coins. Let the chidren make rubbings of the coins, both back and front, by putting thin paper over a coin and crayoning over the top.

Children cut out the purse, coins and labels on an activity sheet. Stick the coins on the inside of the purse and label. Fold the purse on the centre line to close and bend the clasp. Decorate inside the purse.

Ask the children to ask grandparents if they have any pre-decimal coins and make a class display. Look at the dates on the coins and make a timeline. Examine the coins and discuss the different monarchs. Find out more about the farthing and ten shilling and pound notes. What did they look like?

29 Gran and Grandad at Play

Carefully study the two photographs of the boy and girl playing. Talk about what they are doing and if they look as though they are having fun. Ask how the children can tell the photographs are old and to comment on the clothes of the period. The children then complete the activity sheet by drawing and writing about their favourite pastimes.

Encourage the children to ask their grandparents about the games they played at home or in the playground and make a list of those that are the same and those that are different to those they themselves play.

30 Make a 1950's Card Game

This is an opportunity for the children to make and use a card game from the 1950's and can be used as a class/group activity. Discuss the 'old-fashioned' characters on the cards and encourage comment.

Enlarge the page onto A3 - you will need three copies - and stick onto thick card. Cut out the cards and colour, making sure that the same characters are coloured exactly alike, and laminate. Let the children play a 'noisy' game of SNAP in groups of two/three.

31 Party Time - Make Blancmange

Enlarge the photograph and use it as a basis for discussion for birthday celebrations, now and then. Background notes give information on children's parties in the 1950's and 1960's. Discuss the party venue, the ages of the children and the

page

clothes they are wearing, and then make comparisons with the different ways children celebrate their birthdays now. Talk about different venues, party clothes and party food.

Explain that blancmange was a special treat, served usually with jelly, as a sweet to follow sandwiches. Children could follow the recipe and make blancmange. Ask the children the question, "Would you prefer jelly and blanc-mange or burger and chips?"

Children could also follow the recipe (in background notes) and make the peppermint creams.

32 In Days Gone By-
Make a Zig-Zag Story Book

Encourage the children to talk to their grandparents about their childhood and collect and discuss their findings. Enlarge the page onto A3 and let the children choose which grandparent they would like to write about. Children cut carefully around the template and use it to write about Gran/Grandad's childhood memories. These could be displayed alongside photographs of the children's grandparents, when they were young and as they are now. The children could go on to draw large portraits of their grandparents and put them into a class book.

Key Vocabulary

old, new, before, after, present, past, fifty years ago, 1950's, 1960's, young, old, older, memories, childhood, photographs, family tree, old-fashioned, handmade, blancmange, knitting/sewing patterns, homemade, blackboard and easel, pen-nib, counting frame.

Additional Activities

1 Make a collection of everyday objects, e.g. portable radio, hairdryer, shoes, and display with a modern equivalent.

2 Investigate home entertainment – radios, television, computers. What can you find out about the television programmes your grandparents watched? Draw and paint pictures of 'Muffin the Mule' and 'Pinky and Perky'.

3 Learn some children's songs from the 1950's and 1960's.'

Grandad's Timeline

Here are some photographs of me. They show me at different ages in my life. Can you put them in the correct order and label them?

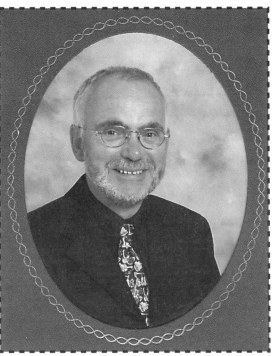

Here I am as a toddler. Look at my tricycle.

Here I am as a young man. I am with my wife.

I am 9-years old in this photograph. What do you think of my go-cart?

This is what I look like now. I am the headteacher of a primary school.

What Did Gran Wear?

Here are some paper dolls I played with when I was little. I wore clothes just like these. My granny made them for me. She sewed my coats and dresses and knitted hats, cardigans and gloves.

cut

What Did Grandad Wear?

This is what I wore when I was little. My mother knitted all my jumpers for me.

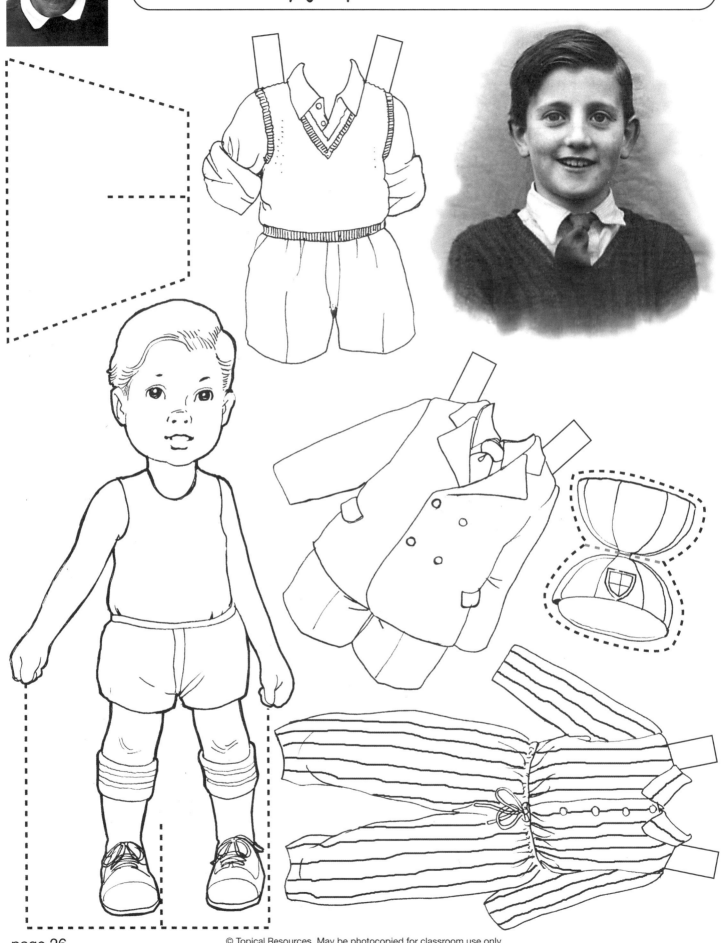

© Topical Resources. May be photocopied for classroom use only.

Grandad at School

Schools were very different when I was a boy. The teachers were very strict and we always worked in silence.

Here I am using a counting frame.

I used a pen with a nib like this to write with.

The teacher used a blackboard and easel.

I had free milk at playtime.

I shared a desk like this. Our desks were in rows.

Make Gran's Purse

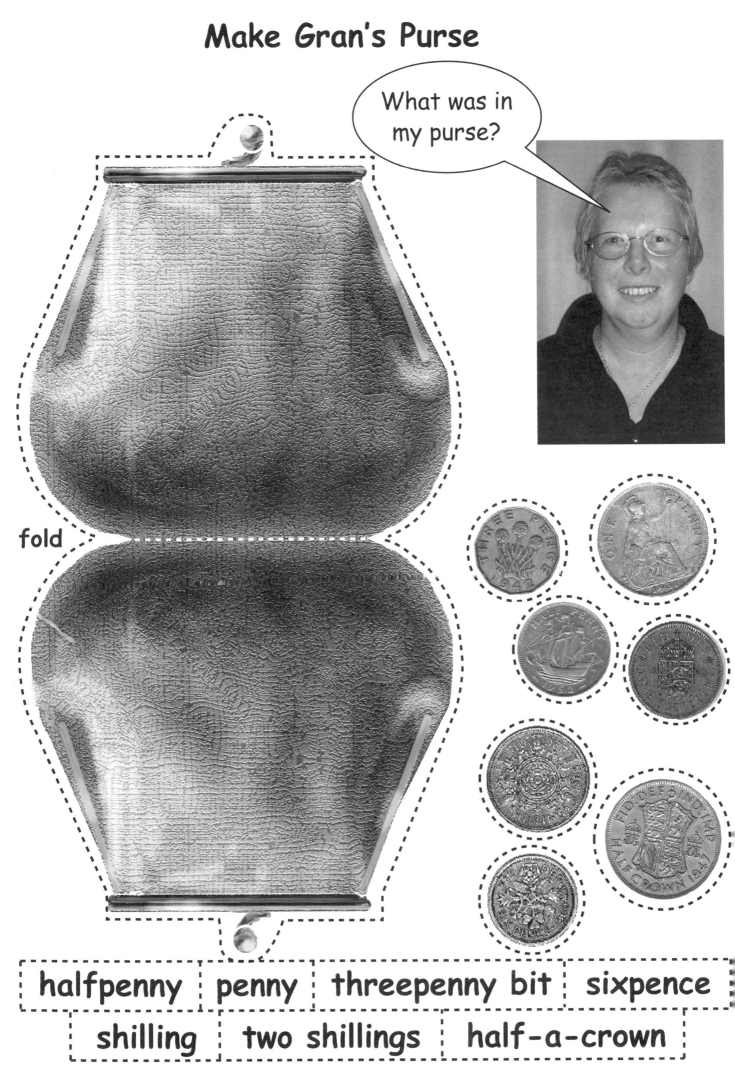

halfpenny · penny · threepenny bit · sixpence

shilling · two shillings · half-a-crown

page 28

Gran and Grandad at Play

Look at the pictures. How can you tell that they are old?

'THEN'

'NOW'

Write and draw about the games that you play with your friends.

Make a 1950's Card Game

I had this card game when I was little. It was good fun to play. Do you think the characters look funny?

Party Time- Make 'Blancmange'

These boys and girls are eating at a birthday party. They are wearing their party clothes. What do you think they are eating and drinking?

'Blancmange' was a great treat at parties when gran and grandad were young. Have you ever eaten it? Try this recipe and see if you like it.

The Recipe

- You need: 75 grams/3 oz. icing sugar, 75 grams/3oz, cornflour, one pint/600mls. milk, milk shake syrup or vanilla essence.

- Mix the icing sugar, corn flour and two tablespoons of milk together to make a paste.

- Boil the rest of the milk and pour into the mixture. Stir well.

- Return to the pan and stir over a gentle heat until the mixture is thick and glossy.

- Add 2-3 tablespoons of milkshake syrup or vanilla essence to flavour and colour.

- Pour into moulds and leave to set.

Write and draw about a birthday party that you have been to. Where was it and what did you wear? Did you have jelly and blancmange?

In Days Gone By - Make a Zig-Zag Story Book

Seaside Holidays - Long Ago

Most of our seaside towns developed and prospered in Victorian times. The advent of the railways meant that hordes of people, both rich and poor, flocked into the resorts. People who lived and worked in the industrial towns now had the opportunity and freedom to visit the seaside, even if only on a 'day trip' to get away from the humdrum of daily life.

Seaside resorts grew up all around the coast of England and Wales, and many of these developed into large towns offering amenities, such as large hotels and boarding houses with the most modern of conveniences. Brighton, Blackpool, Southport, Llandudno, Ilfracombe, Weymouth, Torquay, Dover, Worthing, Hastings, Bournemouth and Scarborough are all examples of towns which became popular in the Victorian and Edwardian eras.

The Victorian and Edwardian attractions were many and varied. The fashionable afternoon promenade was one of the highlights of the day for middle class ladies and gentlemen. This walk to the seafront, along the promenade and to the marina, or about the town was taken by people, dressed in their best, who wanted to see and be seen. A new social venue in many resorts was the 'Winter Gardens', a huge greenhouse like structure, iron-framed and covered in glass. There the gentry wandered among the exotic plants and met to take tea, whilst military style bands entertained the public on bandstands in parks and public gardens. Newly built piers, solid iron-framed structures, extended out into the sea and allowed holiday makers to experience the sea in close proximity without getting wet. These piers often housed the popular music-halls, and were the place for other seaside entertainments such as pierrots and minstrel shows.

New seaside traditions took root in Victorian times. Alongside the simple old-fashioned fun of playing and picnicking on the beach, there were boat trips, Punch and Judy shows, acrobats, travelling photographers, donkey rides and roundabouts. Tasty, informal seaside food became popular and, with little regard for formal manners, cockles, mussels and winkles, fish and chips, ice-cream and candyfloss were all eaten whilst on the move.

Day trips by train or motor coach offered cheap fares and seaside towns became even busier in the 1920's and 1930's. Boarding houses, run by landladies, were the most popular accommodation offered and families often bought their own food for the landladies to cook for tea. Entertainment remained the same, both on and off the beach, with donkey rides, Punch and Judy shows and visits to the funfair. It was a common sight to see older people sitting in rows on the promenade, above the beach in rented deckchairs.

In the 1950's and 1960's more families owned a car and people began to travel to different areas away from the towns and to visit a different resort each year. Campsites, caravan sites and the holiday-camps (such as Butlin's) were in their hey-day. At this time too, holiday companies, such as Cooks, were now offering cheap package holidays to Spain and other continental countries, and many people travelled abroad by plane for the first time.

Postcards

Postcards first came to Great Britain in 1870. They were plain cards issued by the Post Office with a pre-printed stamp. In 1894, private publication was allowed when the Post Office relinquished the monopoly over them. In 1902, the picture postcard, with a divided back, for a message and address, and the picture on the front, was introduced and the size standardised. Everyone used them to send messages and the years between 1902 and 1914 were the 'Golden age of Postcards', as many Edwardians began to collect them as a hobby. At this time the role of the postcard was to extol the virtues of, and advertise, the seaside with scenes of piers, towns, golden beaches and proms etc. The 1930's saw the advent of the saucy postcards with humorous cartoons of big ladies and skinny men, and many of these were printed in Holmfirth, West Yorkshire, by Bamforth and Co. These cards were particularly popular in the 1960's and 1970's. Although the sending of postcards is not as popular now, you can still see the traditional postcard stand or rack outside every seaside gift shop.

Bathing Machines

Bathing machines were first introduced for general use in Scarborough in the 1760's. Queen Victoria had one at Osborne House, Isle of White. Their principal function was to preserve the modesty of the Victorian bather and to allow them to spend the day at the beach in privacy. They varied in style from the luxurious for the rich and royalty to the basic ones to be seen on the majority of beaches. They were made of wood, had steps and small windows and were pulled into the sea by horses.

Swimming Costumes

The Victorians thought their bodies should be covered and in the mid 1800's bathing dresses with long sleeves covered most of the female body and were made of heavy flannel material. These voluminous outfits often had weights sewn into them to stop them from floating and were worn with long bloomers. The men wore all-in-one costumes, which were knee length and elbow length, made of heavy woollen material and often striped. Towards the 1890's, ladies' dresses were knee length with puffed sleeves, usually featuring a sailor collar and made of wool. They were worn over bloomers /drawers trimmed with ribbon or lace. This outfit was accessorised with black stockings, lace-up bathing slippers and pretty bathing caps. By the 1920's an all-in-one above the knee costume was to be seen, although still often worn with stockings and made of heavy material.

As the fashion for a suntan became popular so swimming costumes became smaller, with men wearing trunks and ladies going from costumes that revealed shoulders and thighs to the skimpy bikinis of today.

Holiday Clothes

The Victorian visitors packed large trunks for their holiday. Ladies wore long crinolines, which were later exchanged for bustles. Girls wore their ordinary dresses. Large hats were worn to protect the face from the sun and were made of straw decorated with ribbons. Parasols were carried too. Many paintings illustrate these fashions (e.g. 'Weston Sands' by W. Hopkins and E. Havell, 1864) in City of Bristol Museum and art gallery. Men and boys wore jackets and trousers but began to get a more nautical appearance in the early 1900's when they could be seen in striped jackets, with bright cummerbunds and white flannel trousers, with a straw boater to complete the look.

Punch and Judy

Punch and Judy shows have been popular on the beach since Victorian times. The brightly coloured and distinctive theatre booths were easily dismantled and carried from beach to beach on the back or by cart. The glove puppets were made of wood and cloth, with Mr Punch being the only one with legs and characterised by his big nose and his stick. Mr Punch's voice is spoken through a 'swazzle', which is made of two pieces of metal with cloth in the middle. When you blow through it the cloth vibrates and makes a high sound. The swazzle is held by the puppeteer at the back of his throat. Other characters were Judy and the baby, the policeman, crocodile with his sausages, a ghost and devil, although some of these have changed over the years. The early shows were more for adults and were quite violent but have been modified in recent times.

Seaside Holidays - Long Ago

page

35 Finding Out - a Questionnaire

As an introduction to the topic invite a grandparent or elderly person into the classroom to talk to the children about his/her childhood seaside holidays. Have available photographs, souvenirs and pictures to refer to during the visit. Children use the questionnaire on the activity page to lead the discussion and to record the answers. Encourage them to ask further questions. The children could fill the questionnaire in at home with a parent/grandparent/elderly friend. Use the answers to make lists of popular resorts, seaside pastimes etc. of previous generations and compare with their own holidays.

36 Find the Seaside Towns

Teacher's background notes give information on the growth and development of seaside resorts in Great Britain. How can the children tell they are old? Look at the transport and clothes. Are there any modern amusements? Do they give a clue to what holidays used to be like? Suggested activities include: enlarge a copy of the map on page 62, locate the places and pinpoint them on the map. Encourage the children to bring in postcards old/new, add to the map and label 'Now' and 'Then.' Ask the children to design a poster for one of the seaside towns on the postcards. The children could make a scrap book of postcards they have collected.

37 Design and Write a Postcard

Refer to the postcards old and new that the children have collected. Discuss the scenes and the information they convey. Examine the layout of the back of the postcards. Note where the address and stamp are. Read and discuss the messages. The aim of the activity is for the children to use their knowledge to design a seaside postcard, past or present, on the template at the top of the page and fill in their address and, write a message to a family member on the one below.

38 Make a Victorian Beach Scene

Discuss the background information about Victorian swimwear and bathing machines. Examine photographs and pictures of Victorian seaside scenes. To make the beach scene, sponge-paint a background of sea, sand and sky. Give each child an activity sheet. Colour the bathing machines in bright colours, cut

out and stick onto the background in the sea. Colour and cut out the Victorian lady and gentleman and stick in place on the steps of the bathing machines or in the sea. You can segregate the men and women! Draw and cut out some horses to add to the picture. Alternatively, make a 3D model using the stands provided.

An exciting extension to the activity would be to take a digital photograph of the children and super-impose their faces onto the bathers, thus making them become a part of the Victorian beach scene.

39 Make a Timeline - Swimming Costumes

Enlarge the pictures and use for shared discussion. Point out the dates of the costumes, highlighting the differences and changes, and help the group to sequence the photographs. Cut out the pictures and arrange in order on a time-line, and add an appropriate sentence for each. Encourage the children to bring in photographs from home of grandparents /parents and themselves in swimming costumes and add to the timeline.

40 Pack a Bag - A Cut and Stick Activity

The aim of the activity is to give the children an insight into the clothes that an Edwardian lady/girl might have packed in her bag and to make comparisons with what they put into their suitcase nowadays. Teacher's background notes give some information on seaside clothes. Ask the children, 'What do you wear when you are at the seaside?' Examine paintings and photographs of Edwardian families at the seaside, drawing their attention to the styles of dress and encourage comment, making comparisons with the present day. Children colour and cut out the pictures, together with the labels. Stick the bag onto a piece of paper and put the articles in the bag and label. Give the children an outline of a suitcase and ask them to draw and label the things they would take.

This would be a good time to talk about protection from the sun, with hats and sun-cream etc.

41 Punch and Judy- Make Puppets

Teacher's background notes give information on the development of

Punch and Judy Shows. Have available photographs and pictures of Punch and Judy puppets and theatres, past and present, and discuss the appearance of the characters etc.

Follow the instructions on the activity page to make a Mr. Punch, or choose one of the other characters and make in the same way.

42 Make a Punch and Judy Theatre

Examine the photograph on the activity page and compare with pictures and photographs from the past.

Photocopy activity page on to A3 card. Cut out and fold shape to make a theatre booth. Decorate in an old-fashioned style or like the modern one in the photograph. The children could go on to devise their own Punch and Judy show, using funny voices for Mr Punch and his catchphrase "That's the way to do it."

Alternatively, make a large classroom Punch and Judy Theatre using cardboard boxes. Use pieces of lace, fringing and ribbon to decorate around the stage. Use fabric and string to make curtains. Finally, paint your theatre in stripes using bright colours.

Key Vocabulary

Victorian, Edwardian, 1950's, before, after, now, then, long ago, recent, modern, past, present, old-fashioned, entertainment, souvenirs, postcards, posters, steam train, amusements, cockles and whelks, pier, promenade, Punch and Judy show, parasol, crinoline, bustle, bathing dress, straw-boater, bathing machine, travelling bag.

Additional Activities

1 Investigate seaside snacks, (whelk stands, ice-cream sellers, candy floss, etc.) Find out about seaside rock and how it is made.

2 Make a collection of seaside souvenirs for display in the classroom.

3 Make comparisons of modes of travel, past and present, to seaside venues.

4 Make the creative play area into a travel agent's shop and decorate with seaside posters.

Finding Out... A Questionnaire

I asked .... these questions.

1 When you were little did you go to the seaside?

....

2 Where did you go for your holiday?

....

3 Where did you sleep on holiday ?

....

....

4 What amusements were on the promenade?

....

....

5 Did you go on any rides?

....

....

6 What clothes did you take with you?

....

7 Can you tell me anything else about your seaside holiday?

....

Find The Seaside Towns

Here are some old postcards of different seaside towns. Cut them out and put them in the correct place on your map.

Clovelley 1948

Skegness 1949

Weymouth 1939

Pwllheli 1938

Blackpool 1938

Design and Write a Postcard - 'NOW' or 'THEN'

My postcard is

Write a message to someone special and put their name and address on the postcard.

POST CARD

Address

Make a Victorian Beach Scene

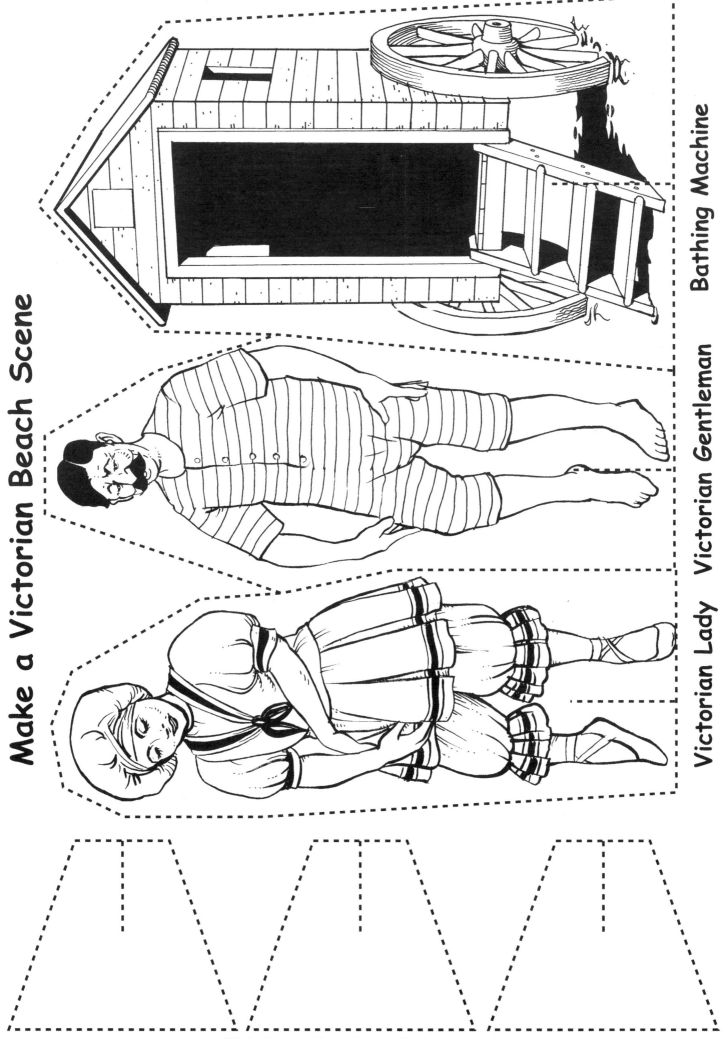

Bathing Machine

Victorian Gentleman

Victorian Lady

Timeline of Swimming Costumes on the Beach

1985

1940

1925

1950

1955

1935

1990

1970

Pack a Bag - A Cut and Stick Activity

Here is a lady's travelling bag from long ago. These are some of the things that she might have taken on holiday. Cut them out. Put them in the bag and label them.

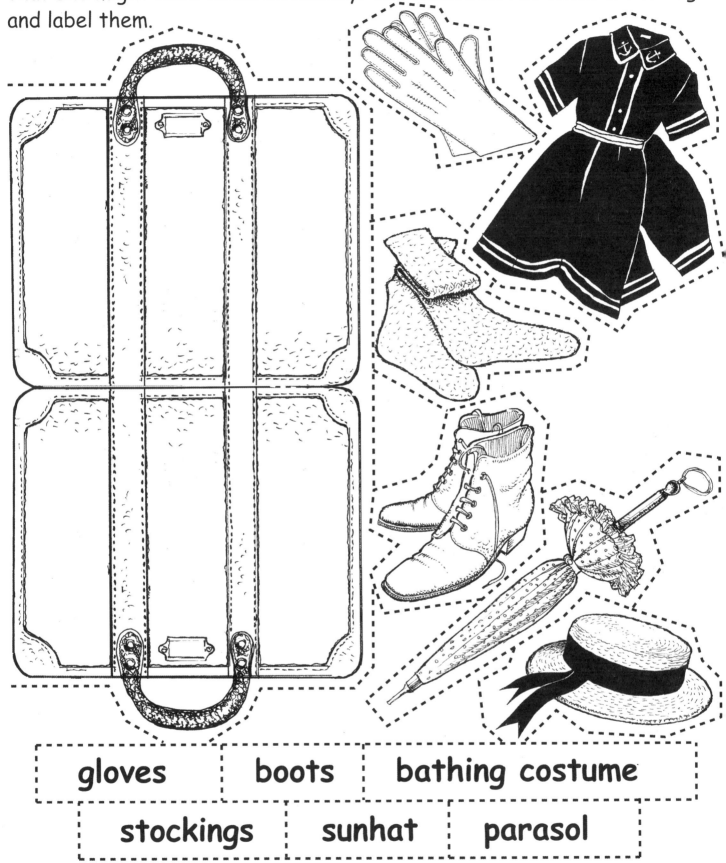

gloves   boots   bathing costume

stockings   sunhat   parasol

Do you think girls and boys would have taken the same things? Now, make a case and put in the things you would take on holiday.

Make Your Own Punch and Judy Puppets

In the past lots of children would gather on the beach to watch a Punch and Judy show. You can still see Mr Punch and his friends making people laugh at some seaside resorts today.

Fold a piece of card in half. Draw happy Mr. Punch on one side. Cut out.

Draw a cross face on the other side. Colour both sides in bright colours.

Glue the Mr Punch faces together with the stick in the middle.

You can make some of the other puppets in the same way.

Judy

Toby

Crocodile

Policeman

Butcher

Make a Punch and Judy Theatre

Here is a picture of a Punch and Judy theatre.

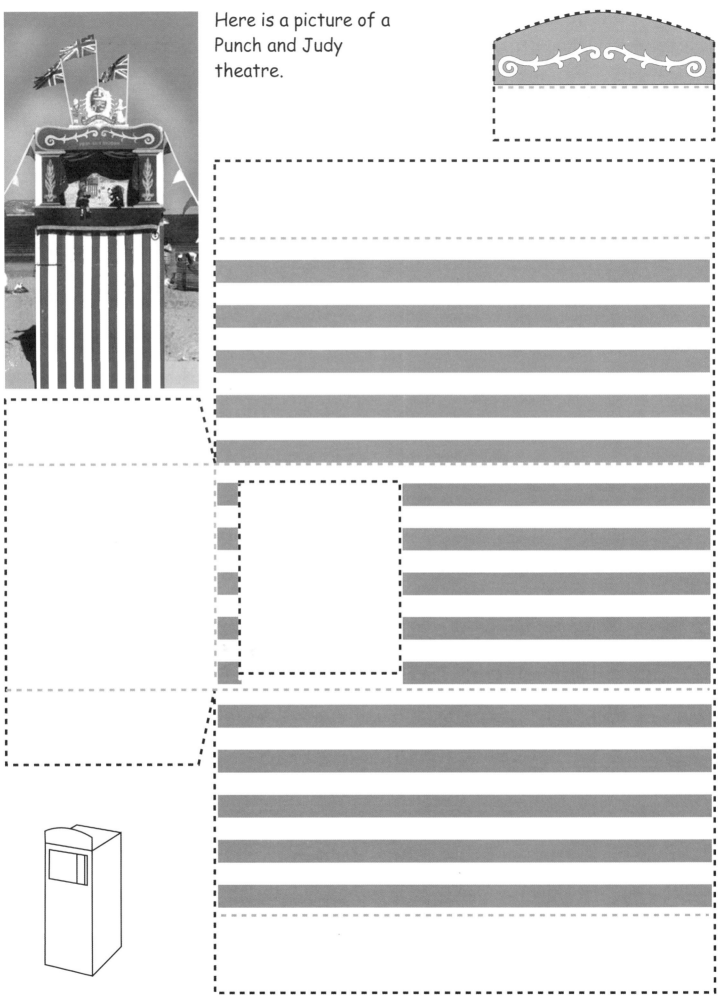

Homes - 'Now' & 'Then'

This unit will help children to develop an understanding of how man has provided shelter and warmth during the last hundred years. Technology has improved the way of life for the majority of people, allowing for a completely different lifestyle with less demand on heavy physical activity which was necessary in all aspects of looking after the home at the beginning of the twentieth century. In towns and cities many of the poor lived in terraced houses, thousands of which had been built cheaply at the end of Victoria's reign.

Some houses were built around square courtyards. The very cheapest houses were built 'back-to-back' where they shared both side and back walls, thus only entering the house by a front door. Many homes did not have water piped into their houses. It was bought from a stand-pipe in the street. Some people would obtain water from wells and streams – therefore it was difficult to keep clean. Poor people would have a shared lavatory in the courtyard or in the alley way. They were not flush toilets and the contents were tipped into cess pits, emptied by the night-soil men. In 1875, a Public Health Act forced councils to build sewers and provide safe water supplies as an increasing number of people died from typhus and cholera due to the filthy conditions in which they lived. Towns and cities grew quickly as people sought work in new factories and mills. Some working-class people kept their homes clean and as comfortable as was within their means. The very worst conditions were for those who could only afford to rent a room or cellar. People were crammed together in unsanitary conditions with perhaps only one tap for a hundred people. Thousands of people lived in these slums in the towns and cities.

In rural areas, farm workers often lived in tied cottages that went with the job. The condition of the cottages varied. Some were well maintained by their landlords, others were damp and had only earth floors. A privy at the bottom of the garden could be shared by several families.

There were others more fortunate where a man was able to provide a very comfortable life for his wife and family. If he earned £1000 a year he could afford a large house with servants. Many girls left their homes in the country to go into service in the towns. Servants worked long hours often involved in heavy physical work - washing, ironing and cooking so that the lady of the house could engage in more gentle pursuits and leisure activities. Such women had no opportunity to follow a career. The very rich could afford a house in town and also ran an estate in the country.

Children will be able to compare the lives of people in the past with the way we live today. For example, washday even fifty years ago could take all day - using a mangle and washtub which was labour intensive.

Before the common use of the electric iron, ironing was undertaken with flat irons.

Additional Activities

1. Make a model of a room eg. a modern dining room, using a shoe box. Now make a comparative model of the same room 50 years ago.

2. Look at styles of windows, doors and chimneys. Compare the different styles.

3. Turn the home corner into a bedroom or a living room of long ago.

4. Make a museum – bring in artefacts from long ago.

   Write captions beside each artefact. Draw up a catalogue of all the items and invite visitors to look around your museum.

5. Collect pictures of the homes of people in other countries. Discuss why they may be different.

A classroom display about homes

Homes - 'Now' & 'Then'

pages

45 Homes - 'Old' and 'New'

The photographs on the activity page will introduce children to some of the kinds of houses they will see in the city town and countryside. Look at the differing external features of the houses on the activity pages.

The rural cottage has been enlarged and changed over time.

The semi-detached is a mid thirties home, built from brick, with leaded windows at the front of the house.

The brick detached house, built in the 1990's, shows a double detached garage.

Terraced houses were built cheaply at the end of the 19th century and beginning of the 20th century. Cut out the pictures and stick them into a book entitled, 'All about Houses'. Encourage children to collect pictures of houses from magazines and calendars. Add these to the book and write captions under each house.

46 Changes in a 100 Years?

Compare the two house interiors - both showing a kitchen. How are they different? Cut out the captions '100 years ago in the kitchen' and 'Now in the kitchen' (or write your own). Stick each caption at the top of a sheet of A4 paper. Cut out and stick the pictures of implements used in the home in the appropriate columns. Ask children to bring artefacts to form a display about long ago in the home.

47 Houses Can be Different

Discuss the differences in the modern and the Victorian house. Cut out and then sort the pieces of the two jigsaws to complete the modern and Victorian house. Stick the pictures into your book about houses and write about the differences between the two exteriors. Reference can be made to the activity on page 46.

pages

48 Bedrooms - 'Now' and 'Then'

The two bedrooms show the changes over 100 years. Ask the children to observe the differences. How comfortable would an iron bedstead/straw-filled mattress be? Would you prefer to use a bathroom or the potty and the ewer (large jug) and basin (often the water was frozen in winter.) People often utilised old clothes to make rag rugs and patch work quilts. Handmade lace and samplers took up much spare time and were often worked by a dimly lit candle. Think about the safety aspects of candles and oil lamps. Through discussion be aware of the changes in technology. Make lists of articles which are no longer in general use.

49 Sort out the Bedrooms

Fold a piece of A4 paper (landscape style) into three with the titles 100 years ago, 50 years ago and Now. Cut out the pictures and stick them correctly into the first 2 columns. In the third column draw articles which are in your bedroom. e.g. computers, televisions, etc.

50 Homes - What Did Artists See?

The painting, 'Washing Day' introduces children to a family engaged in the whole day activity of washing in the late nineteenth century. The day was labour intensive with water to be boiled, clothes scrubbed by hand, clothes hung up indoors to steam and dry on wet days and later to air after ironing.

A mangle was often used (see picture on page 46) Mother would work hard all day. By contrast, as shown in the lithograph 'New Baby' a more well to do family of the same period would have servants to help with household tasks. The baby would have been looked after by a nursery maid. A cook would have prepared the meals for the family and a servant would have cleaned the house. After discussion suggested activities are:

Make a concertina book entitled, 'Work in the home long ago'.

Paint comparative pictures – washing day in the nineteenth century and today. Discuss - 'Is it really washing day any more?'

pages

51 Make a Model Street Scene

Invite the children to make a list of as many types as of houses as they can. Use the photographs on the activity page to help make a collection of miniature houses. (The pictures could be enlarged if desired). Cut out each picture and stick it onto the front of a box. The boxes could be made into a street scene. The aim of the activity is for children to learn that a typical street has developed over time with different types of housing. For example a house may be pulled down and replaced by a block of flats. Create gardens in front of the houses where appropriate. Make a pavement and road out of paper. Use any street furniture available to enliven the scene e.g. toy cars, lamp posts, traffic lights and trees. Find other pictures of houses and stick them onto boxes to make a longer street. Cut out and place the family on to the street scene.

Key Vocabulary

Victorian, modern, detached, semi-detached, cottage, terraced, mansion, flats, caravan, flat iron, wash stand, mangle, posser, modern kitchen implements, electricity.

Homes 'Old' and 'New'

Look at the photographs of the houses. How are they different? Cut out the pictures and stick them into a book called, 'All About Houses. Say how each house is different. Now draw your house and then the house of a friend.

Changes in 100 Years

100-years ago in the kitchen   NOW in the kitchen

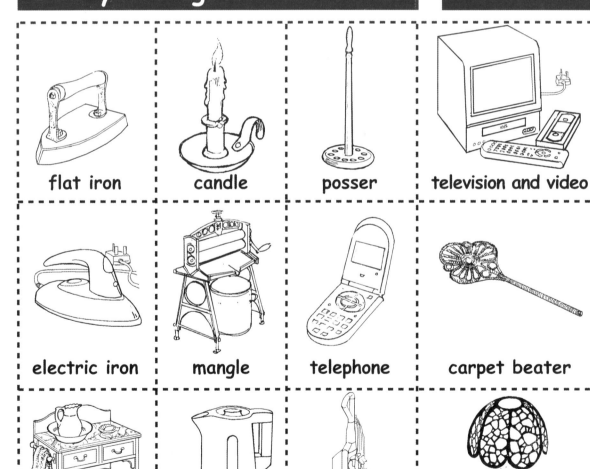

flat iron	candle	posser	television and video	dolly tub
electric iron	mangle	telephone	carpet beater	washer
wash stand	electric kettle	vacuum cleaner	electric lamp	microwave

Houses Can Be Different

Sort out the pieces and make two jigsaws. One is a Victorian house and one is a modern house. How are the two houses different? Write and draw about the differences.

Bedrooms 'NOW' and 'THEN'

A bedroom 100 years ago. Would you like to sleep in it?

100 Years Ago

Here is a bedroom 50 years ago. Can you see any differences?

50 Years Ago

Sort Out The Bedrooms

Homes - What Did Artists See?

Washing Day painted by
Pierre Edouard Frere in 1878

Often farm workers' cottages were damp and roofs let in water.

The water to wash in came from a village pump or well.

How is the washing done in your house?

New Baby lithographed in 1880

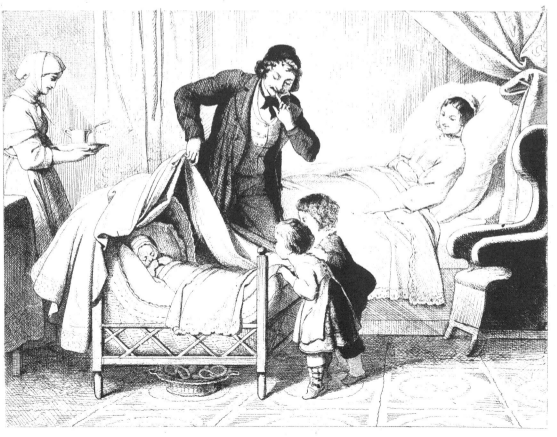

The family are admiring the new baby.

The baby was looked after by a nanny in the nursery.

They had a young servant who helped cook the meals, lay the fires and do the washing.

Make A Model Street Scene

People live in many different kinds of houses – flats, bungalows, caravans, mansions, detached houses, terraced houses... Can you think of any more? Cut out the pictures and stick each home on to the front of a box. Find other pictures and make a collection of miniature homes.

A Bungalow

A Block of Flats

A Semi-Detatched House

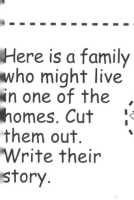

Here is a family who might live in one of the homes. Cut them out. Write their story.

A Caravan

Castles - Long Ago

A castle was built by the king to guard a ford or crossing place or to protect a town. Castles were also built on the coast to guard against invasion. However, most castles were built by barons and knights to be their homes and differed according to why they were built. It was the home of the king and a centre for his soldiers. Castles could be used by barons to protect land given to them by the king. They were first built just prior to the time of the Normans and continued for a further 400 years.

Motte and Bailey Castles

Pre 1066 some castles were built in preparation for invasion. They were known as 'Motte and Bailey' Castles. The Motte or mound was made from earth and on it was built a wooden tower or keep for the garrison. The bailey was the courtyard at the bottom of the mound and housed the livestock. It was surrounded by a ditch and later a moat. The first castles were constructed with wood as there wasn't the time to quarry the stone required. The palisades of sharpened stakes could be thrown up quickly.

William the Conqueror

William, whose father was Robert Duke of Normandy, was a strong and robust baby. His mother Herleva, was the daughter of a humble tanner. His father died when William was seven. The young child often had to escape from his home in the middle of the night as many wanted to kill him. By the age of 25 he had taken control of Normandy and cast his eye across the Channel. The saintly English King, Edward the Confessor was growing old and was more interested in building Westminster Abbey than ruling England. In 1064 Earl Harold, the most powerful man in England, was caught in a storm and captured in France. William ordered his release and welcomed him but made him swear to help William to become king of England when Edward died. King Harold Hardrada, King of Norway also wanted the throne and thus set sail, landed and was joined by Harold's brother, Tostig with whom he had quarrelled and wanted revenge. Harold marched to Stamford Bridge, his promise forgotten, where Hardrada and Tostig were killed. Meanwhile William had landed in Hastings and Harold had to move his weary troops south to fight before they had time to rest. Within three weeks they were fighting William, a battle which was to last all day. Harold was hit by an arrow in his eye so the popular story goes. The Saxons had lost their leader and William became king of England.

The Bayeux Tapestry

The tapestry was woven in England by English embroiders in Canterbury on the orders of Bishop Odo of Bayeux (William's brother-in-law). It was made with woollen thread on a linen background and was finally finished in France. It tells the story of the preparations for and Battle of Hastings. Over the centuries it has had a chequered history- lost, stolen and restored many times. Now it is a major tourist attraction. In 1729 Antoine Benoit carried out a full scale tracing as a basis for an engraving. In 1819 Charles Stothard prepared another set of facsimile prints. With the advent of the camera another record was made in 1872. In each of these records there were many variations. Perhaps most important the slaying of Harold differs. In the 1729 depiction the king is seen grasping a spear which he is either trying to throw or pull out. By 1819 the shaft has feathers on it and in 1872 the arrow is pointing to the King's right eye but hidden by the nosepiece of his helmet. The nature of Harold's death is unclear. Evidence points to a hit squad sent by William to despatch the king, although he had previously declared he would kill him in combat. Perhaps he wanted to be sure! Harold's body was badly mutilated. William probably felt that his victory had been dishonoured as he sent the culprit home in disgrace having stripped him of his knighthood.

Norman Rule

William tried a conciliatory approach but due to regular insurrections he was forced to subdue the population wherever there was discontent. Once they were subjugated, William built castles to stop future problems. During his 21 years reign he built 100 castles.

The Domesday Book gives a picture of English society on the eve of the Norman conquest and then again twenty years later. It was a massive survey into the state of William's recently acquired kingdom and recorded in two volumes called Great and Little Domesday. Each manor was described at the time of the conquest and then again in 1086. From the Domesday accounts, historians have been able to show how people lived, the agricultural conditions and social customs. Of greatest interest perhaps for the children is the description of the people Domesday describes. There were great bishops, earls and barons who had great estates and in return promised loyalty to the king, including military help in war. The lords had to pay for the services of armed and mounted knights. The lord of the manor owned a small estate, often with a village attached to it. 'Freemen' held land and paid rent to the lord whilst the 'villeins' were smallholders who did not own their land but paid for it by working for the lord of the manor. Worst off were the slaves who owned nothing but worked for food and shelter. The 'cottars' or cottagers worked for the lord and could not move away.

Additional activities

1 Draw a plan of your ideal castle making sure it has plenty of defences.

2 Make a model of a village outside the castle walls.

3 Draw pictures of the people who lived in the village.

Castles - Long Ago

page

54 The First Castles

Refer to the information in the Teacher's Background Notes to introduce the topic and then read 'The First Castles' as a shared text. Look carefully at the words highlighted and discuss their meanings. Make a castle in a sand tray and label the important features. Begin a book entitled, 'Life in a Castle'.

55 Defending a Castle

The provision of pictures and books will help children to study the defence of castles. Read the captions under the boxes on the activity sheet and with the help of books carefully draw appropriate pictures (see drawings below).

56 Using Evidence - What Happened in 1066?

Let the children study the given section of the Bayeux Tapestry and discuss what they think is happening. Tell the story of 1066 – William hears from his spies that Harold has taken the throne and crowned himself King of England. William builds boats in preparation for invasion. The incident on the activity page shows the French and English in deadly combat. When Harold is killed, William claims the throne. After discussion make a class collage of an incident from the tapestry. Draw portraits of William and Harold. Draw William landing in England in the same style as the illustration on the activity page. Talk about our present monarch.

57 Put the Castles on the Map

Enlarge and cut out the map on page 62. Cut out the pictures of the castles separately and, as a class activity, pin or stick the castles on the map. Discuss the castles which were built in different periods:

The Tower of London – Built in 1078 as a symbol of William's power – 'a fortress for his defence, and a prison for his enemies'. It was completed 20 years later and included a chapel, guardroom, crypts and was protected by a wide ditch. It became a museum in 1603 when James I ordered the crown jewels to be kept in The Tower.

Ludlow Castle - built in 1083 on cliffs overlooking the River Teme. It became one of the most strategic fortifications on the Welsh border, the keep and the inner bailey being the oldest parts of the castle. The keep was known as the Great Tower, the moat was never filled with

page

water. The inner bailey is now used for tourist events.

Conway Castle - built by Edward 1 in 1283 is oblong in shape with three drum towers and thick walls. The village beside it was fortified by a strong wall, 21 towers and 3 gates. The castle and town are now popular visitor attractions.

Deal Castle - is situated on the seafront of the Kentish town of Deal. It was commissioned by Henry V111 in the late 1530's. During the Civil War in 1648 it was besieged but never engaged in military action. It is one of the finest artillery works in England, built to protect the Downs Anchorage and the Kentish coast.

Collect pictures of other castles to put on the map.

58 Design Your Own Coat of Arms

Talk about the knight on the activity sheet with his coat of arms. Use the template to design your own coat of arms using the rule that only red, blue, black, green, purple, silver and gold may be used.

59 Life in a Castle

Talk about the lives and work of the people who lived in a castle. Using the activity sheet let the archer, blacksmith and the lord with his lady tell their own story in the speech bubbles. Continue with the book entitled, 'Life in a Castle', and stick the characters in your book. Now research other people who worked in the castle and add them to your book, letting them tell their own story.

60 Feasting

Discuss all the activities illustrated on this page and compare to a party which you have attended. What are the similarities and differences? Draw pictures with speech bubbles for the jester, musician and servant and add them to your book, 'Life in a Castle'. Find an occasion to have a party to make a direct comparison. Make the play corner into a 'party time area' and have fun serving party food to the dolls and teddies – and yourselves, of course!

61 A Strange Feast

Recite the poem, 'Four and twenty black birds baked in a pie.' Talk about the strange pies that were made in medieval times using birds from the size of a sparrow to a swan. Read the recipe on the activity page as a shared text. Utilize the teaching assistant or willing helper

page

to make - 'A tart of apples and oranges.' Show the children the ingredients. Ask an adult to boil the water, honey and lemon juice and then let the children see how the mixture has changed after boiling. The pie could then be made by a small group of children with an adult's help. Enact the scene when the pie is carried into the feast.

Key Vocabulary

Castles, motte, bailey, palisade, moat, keep, drawbridge, battering-ram, portcullis, slit-windows, turrets, battlements, feast, knight, coat-of-arms, Bayeux Tapestry.

The First Castles

The first castles were built on a hill called a 'motte'. A 'keep' was built on the top of the hill. The Lord and Lady lived in the keep. At the bottom of the motte was a 'bailey' or courtyard. Villagers lived with their animals in the bailey. Often a fence or 'palisade' surrounded both the motte and the bailey. Castle builders often dug a ditch or 'moat' around the motte and bailey. The 'drawbridge' was the only way into the castle.

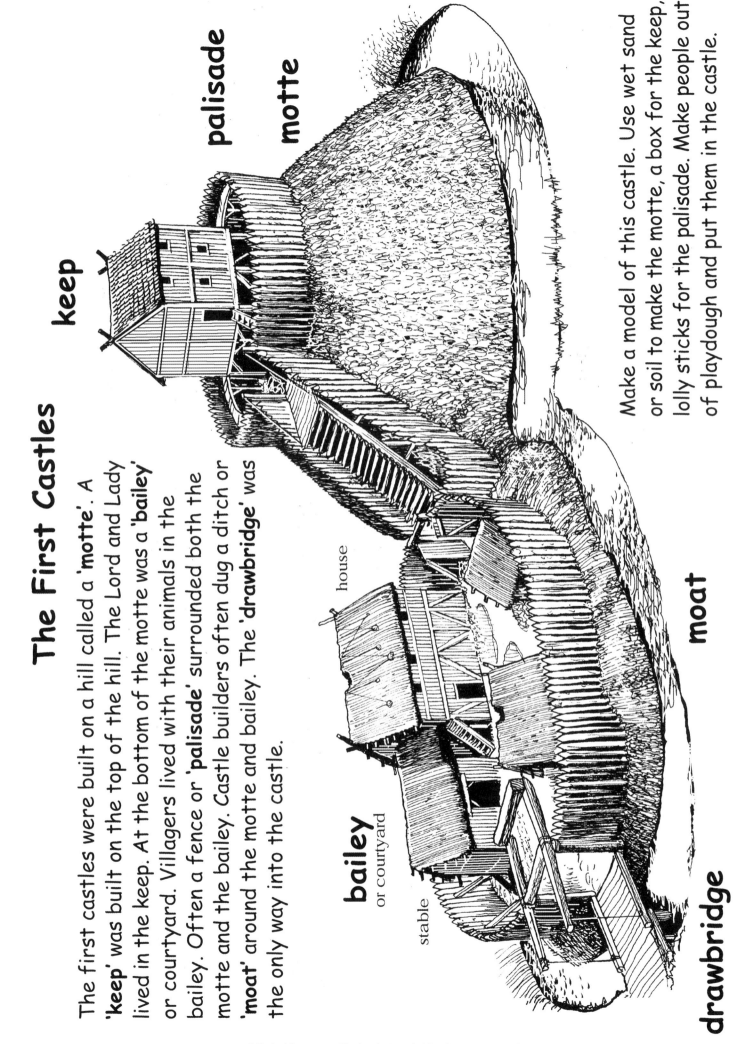

keep

palisade

motte

house

bailey
or courtyard

stable

moat

drawbridge

Make a model of this castle. Use wet sand or soil to make the motte, a box for the keep, lolly sticks for the palisade. Make people out of playdough and put them in the castle.

Defending A Castle

Many castles were built with stone. Here are some ways in which a castle could be defended. Draw your own pictures.

The Lord of the castle and his family lived in the keep – the safest part of the castle.

Over the moat was a drawbridge which was raised in times of danger.

Doors were very strong to protect them against battering rams.

The inner gate was protected by a portcullis.

Narrow slit windows protected the archers from enemy fire.

The turrets on the high walls gave space to shoot through and walls to hide behind.

Heavy stones and hot water were thrown from the battlements onto the enemy.

The enemy sometimes tried to tunnel under the castle walls.

1066- What happened?

What is happening in this part of the Bayeux Tapestry?
What happened before this event? What happened after this event?

Put The Castle On The Map

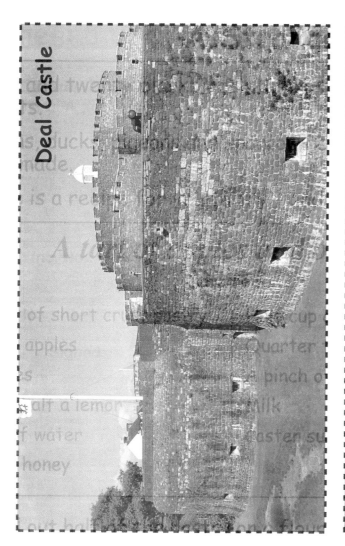

Deal Castle

Conway Castle

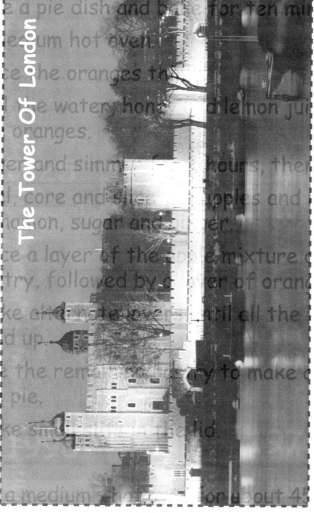

The Tower Of London

Ludlow Castle

Design Your Own Coat Of Arms

I am a knight, ready for battle. Look at my armour and my helmet with a vizor. Nobody will recognise me so I have my personal coat of arms on my shield. I am only allowed 7 colours on my family's coat of arms. They are red, blue, black, green, purple, silver and gold.

Design your own coat of arms. Which colour will you use?

Life In A Castle

I am an archer

I am the blacksmith

I am a knight with my lady

Feasting

Have you been to a party? How is this feast different?

Find the Lord, the jester, the musician and a servant.

Who else can you see?

People ate from a trencher - a one-day old piece of bread.

They used a knife and spoon. Forks had not been invented.

A Strange Feast

'Four and twenty blackbirds', tells us what strange food was eaten at feasts.

Swans, ducks, pigeons and sparrows could be put in pies. Fruit pies were also made.

Here is a recipe for you to try - and then you too can have a feast.

A tart of apples and oranges

Ingredients:

1 packet of short crust pastry
4 eating apples
4 oranges
Juce of half a lemon
3 cups of water
1 cup of honey

Half cup of brown sugar
Quarter teaspoon cinnamon
A pinch of dried ginger
Milk
Caster sugar

1. Roll out half of the pastry on a floured board.
2. Line a pie dish and bake for ten minutes in a medium hot oven.
3. Slice the oranges thinly.
4. Boil the water, honey and lemon juice, add the oranges.
5. Cover and simmer for 2 hours, then drain.
6. Peel, core and slice the apples and mix with cinnamon, sugar and ginger.
7. Place a layer of the apple mixture onto the pastry, followed by a layer of oranges.
8. Make alternate layers until all the fruit is used up.
9. Use the remaining pastry to make a lid for the pie.
10. Make small slits in the lid.

A pie is carried into a feast in a castle

Bake in a medium – hot oven for about 45 minutes.

Great Britain

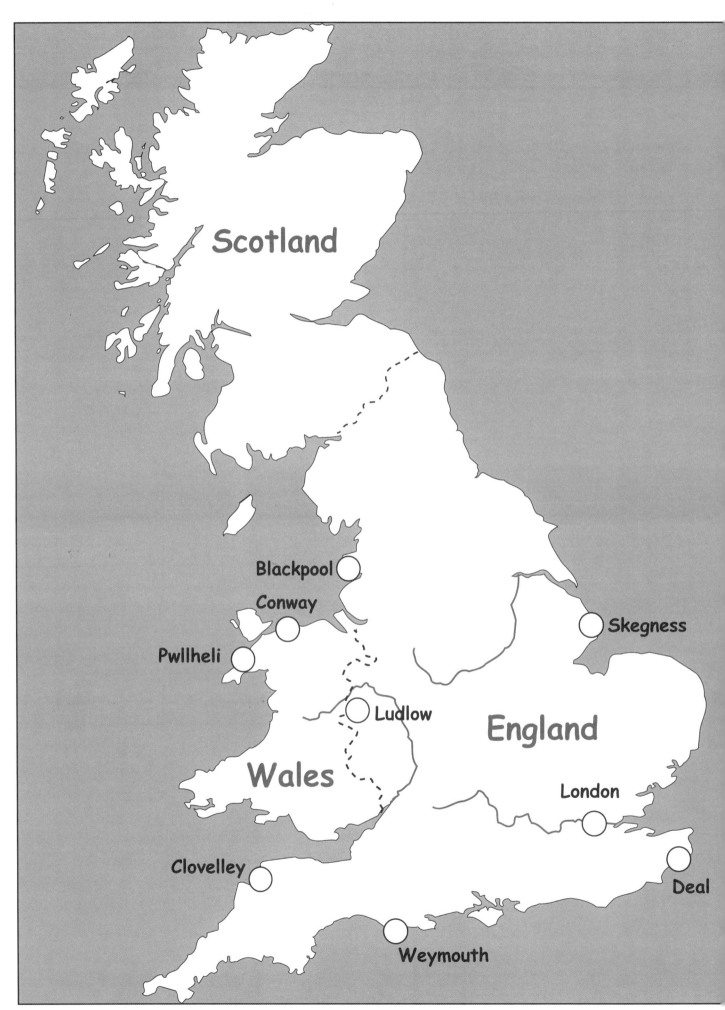

Scotland

Blackpool

Conway

Pwllheli

Skegness

Ludlow

England

Wales

London

Clovelley

Deal

Weymouth

Here Are The Most Interesting Things I Have Discovered

I Have Been Learning About

I found out about the following...

1 _____

_____

2 _____

_____

3 _____

_____

The most interesting part was...

_____

_____